More PVC Projects for the Outdoorsman

TOM FORBES

More PVC Projects for the Outdoorsman

Building Inexpensive Shelters, Hunting and
Fishing Gear, and More Out of Plastic Pipe

Paladin Press • Boulder, Colorado

Also by Tom Forbes:
The Invisible Advantage:
         A Step-by-Step Guide to Making Ghillie Suits
         and Custom Camouflage Accessories (video)
The Invisible Advantage Workbook:
         Ghillie Suit Construction Made Simple
Modern Muzzleloading:
         Black Powder Shooting for Sport, Survival,
         and Self-Defense (video)
PVC Projects for the Outdoorsman:
         Building Shelters, Camping Gear, Weapons,
         and More Out of Plastic Pipe

More PVC Projects for the Outdoorsman: Building Inexpensive Shelters, Hunting and Fishing Gear, and More Out of Plastic Pipe
by Tom Forbes

Copyright © 2002 by Tom Forbes

ISBN 1-58160-355-X
Printed in the United States of America

Published by Paladin Press, a division of
Paladin Enterprises, Inc.
Gunbarrel Tech Center
7077 Winchester Circle
Boulder, Colorado 80301 USA
+1.303.443.7250

Direct inquiries and/or orders to the above address.

Visit our Web site at www.paladin-press.com

Contents

Warning

Some of the projects found in this book can be dangerous if used improperly. The author, publisher, and distributors of this book disclaim any liability from any damage or injuries of any type that a reader or user of information contained within this book may incur from the use of said information.

Introduction

If you have bought this book you probably fall into one or more of these categories: outdoorsman, survivalist, do-it-youselfer, or someone who can't pound a nail straight. As for me, I fall into all four.

As you will see by the projects in this book, I love hunting and fishing and making things myself, but I can't pound a nail or cut a board straight to save my soul. A lot of the projects were developed as a way to have fun doing things I enjoy, as well as save a couple bucks, something else I like to do.

True, some of the things in this book could be purchased off the shelf for a few dollars more than it takes to construct them, but that's not really the issue. This book will give you the knowledge and the confidence to do things for yourself.

Many of these projects can be replicated using other materials, such as bamboo and even copper pipe. It's up to you. Just keep safety in mind when building and using these projects; some of these projects can be dangerous if not used carefully.

Good luck and have fun.

Getting Started

CHAPTER 1

TOOLS AND MATERIALS

The tools and materials needed for each project will obviously vary, but here is a list of what you might need for a typical project:

1. PVC pipe (from 1/2-inch CPVC pipe up to 4-inch pipe)
2. Tape measure or yard stick
3. Hacksaw
4. Sandpaper
5. Drill or hobby tool
6. Duct tape
7. Para cord
8. Nylon webbing (like that used in seatbelts, ranging from 1 to 2 inches wide)

9. PVC cleaner
10. PVC cement
11. JB Weld epoxy
12. Silicone chalk
13. Camouflage paint or tape
14. Spray foam insulation
15. Wooden dowels
16. Black permanent marker
17. Finger saw or commando saw
18. Bench vice
19. Various nuts, bolts, and pop rivets

CONSTRUCTION TIPS

Here are a few things to keep in mind during the planning and building stages:

The projects in this book use PVC pipe of various sizes ranging from small 1/2 inch CPVC to 4 inches in diameter with end caps, elbows, T-connectors, and spacers. As a rule use the heavy-walled PVC for these projects. There is a cellulose-lined PVC pipe available now, but while it's cheaper and lighter it is not as durable, so it is best to steer clear of this type.

Use PVC pipe cleaner on all surfaces that will be cemented.

These projects can be painted with any paint that will work on plastic. Make sure the pipe and fittings are clean first, which can be done by simply wiping the pipe down with a damp rag. Camouflage tape also works very well on PVC.

Parts used for some projects may not be readily available; however, since the PVC industry has realized its many different uses, new fittings are always being made available. If the local hardware store does not have what you need, ask them if they have access to furniture fittings made of PVC. If the part you need is still unavailable, you may have to be a bit inventive. For example, several projects use a three-way 90-degree elbow that is the same diameter on all ends. These can be hard to find. If you can't find one, you can get by using a same style of elbow that is threaded on the third opening and attaching the PVC pipe onto a threaded connector.

Many of the projects call for the use of couplers to connect the pipe. A fast and easy alternative to the common external coupler is to make an internal coupler. This can be done by inserting a short piece of wooden dowel that measures the same outside diameter as the internal diameter of the pipe being used. This not only works for extending the length of pipe, but also can strengthen an existing joint. The rafting pole and the pickup shelter are two examples of using an internal coupler.

Cementing the pipe increases a structure's strength, but may mean it's no longer portable (as in large projects such as shelters). The best way to determine whether or not to cement a project together is to decide how portable and how sturdy it needs to be. Many projects can be left uncemented or just cemented at the fittings to allow for easy partial disassembly. In other projects, such as the bow saw and gun rack, cementing the finished project is essential.

As you shop for supplies, you will notice several different styles of end caps. Threaded, unthreaded, external, and internal all have their place. In some case where I have used external caps you may want to use internal caps. Be your own judge as to which will work for you. Since publication of the first book, *PVC Projects for the Outdoorsman*, manufacturers have made both flat and domed end caps in virtually all sizes of pipe.

As you go through this book you will notice that I like to use para cord. Versatile and practical, it not only provides you with a soft grip, but also a very valuable commodity when outdoors—cordage. Knots can be secured by heating them with a match or lighter.

PVC pipe can be made much more rigid by filling the hollow center of the pipe with spray-foam insulation, a wooden dowel, sand, or even concrete.

Always assemble the project completely before cementing. This can save you a lot of grief if something isn't quit right.

Spacers are small lengths of pipe used to connect two fittings. They are usually no more than an inch or two in length depending on the diameter of the pipe and the depth of the fitting.

WORKING WITH TARPS

Many of the projects contained herein are finished with tarps. I like to use nylon tarps because they are cheap, lightweight, durable, come in many colors, and can be used for a lot of different things. The projects in this book use them mostly as shelter covers, but they also make great seats for chairs.

Tarps can be cut and glued or taped to fit shelter frames. Tarp repair kits are cheap and handy to have around. Grommet kits are great for installing grommets to hold the tarp in place. On shelters, once the grommet is set and the lashing cord is in place, glue or tape a piece of tarp over the grommet. This will help keep rain, dust and snow from coming in.

Hunting

CHAPTER 2

MAINSPRING FOR
A SNARE TRAP

Virtually every book on survival or primitive trapping shows how to make a snare trap. This is good information to have, but what do you do if you don't have a springy sapling or tree branch? If this is the situation, you can use 1/2- or 3/4-inch PVC pipe that is either staked down or lashed to a solid object such as a rock or fence post.

Since the shorter the PVC pipe is the more rigid it is, it is best to use only as much as you need; in most cases 6 to 8 feet is plenty.

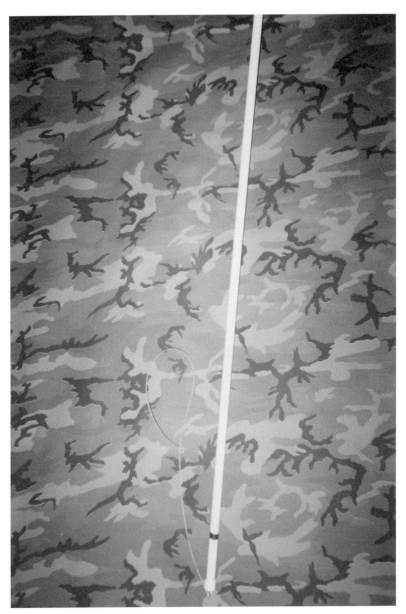

Snare trap mainspring.

Materials

- One 1/2- or 3/4-inch diameter pipe cut to a useable length
- One 1/2- or 3/4-inch diameter end cap
- A length of snare wire with two cable stops. (The cable stops are required by law in most states and prevent the loop of the snare from closing too tightly.)

Instructions

Step 1
Drill a hole through the end cap.

Step 2
Insert the tail end of the snare wire through the hole in the end cap. The length of the snare wire will be determined by the size of the snare loop and the length of wire from the end cap to the top of the snare loop. This will vary based on how high off the ground you wish the loop to be and by the amount of flex or spring you want in the PVC mainspring.

Step 3
Place a cable stop on the wire on the inside of the cap to prevent the wire from sliding out. It you don't have a cable stop, you can use a split shot used in fishing. Slide the split shot around the snare wire and compress it with pliers or give it a good whack with a hammer or stone. Another idea is to loop the wire around a small nail and twist the wire back onto itself.

Step 4
Cement the end cap onto the pipe.
An alternative to this would be to cement a coupler

with a threaded end onto the pipe by drilling a hole though a threaded interior end cap and inserting the wire. The advantage to this is that you can remove the end cap and adjust the length of snare wire, which is not an option when the end cap is cemented into place.

Step 5

Lash the pipe to a secure object such as a fence post or tree.

Step 6

Open the loop to the desired size. Bend the pole over and set the trigger. The trigger will anchor the snare in place until tripped.

Trigger Instructions

A simple trigger can be made by drilling a hole into the side of the pipe. Anchor a stick with a small branch at the top into the ground. (A narrow piece of metal rod would work even better.) Bend the top over at a right angle.

With the pole bent over, insert the small branch or bent piece of rod into the hole. This will hold the pole in place. When the animal is caught by the snare its movement will pull the pole away from the branch or rod, releasing the pole.

There are many different types of triggers, such as the Figure 4 and the notched stake, that will work equally well for this type of spring snare.

SLINGSHOT

Without a doubt this is one of my favorite projects. I have always liked implements of destruction, with a preference for those of a handheld nature. The PVC slingshot is—in my mind—nearly perfect for hunting small rodents or simply putting holes in pop cans.

Materials

- One 7-inch section of 1/2-inch diameter pipe
- Two 3 1/2-inch sections of 1/2-inch diameter pipe
- Two 1-inch sections of 1/2-inch diameter pipe (these will be your spacers)
- One 1/2-inch diameter T-connector
- Two 1/2-inch diameter 90-degree elbows
- Three 1/2-inch diameter end caps
- Rubber bands (Replacement bands can be made from an old bike inner tube. Just ask grandpa, I'll bet he can show you how it's done.)
- Para cord

Instructions

Step 1

Insert the 7-inch section of pipe into the bottom opening of the T-connector. Insert a 1-inch spacer into each of the remaining openings.

Step 2

Attach 90-degree elbows to each of the spacers, both pointing upward. Insert a 3 1/2-inch pipe into the remaining opening of each of the elbows. Place end caps on the ends of the 3 1/2-inch pipe.

The author with his PVC slingshot.

Step 3
Drill a hole through the caps large enough to run your rubber bands through; knot them securely. Be sure to smooth the edges of the holes so there are no sharp edges to wear through the bands. Note: Replacement bands from a sporting goods store will probably have a built-in leather or canvas cradle for the projectile. If you make your own bands, you will have to fashion your own cradle as well.

Step 4
Drill a hole in the remaining end cap and run the para cord through it for a lanyard. Cementing the end cap is optional here. If you do not cement it, you can use the hollow handle to store shot or a spare set of bands.

Make sure the bands are carefully knotted to avoid slippage.

DUCK HUNTER'S SEAT

For the hunter that spends a lot of time sneaking through the marsh after waterfowl, this seat is the perfect accessory. It can be carried over your shoulder and allows you to take a break anywhere. You can build this seat without the hinge, but the hinge allows you to flip the seat up so that it lays flat along the side of the pipe. This makes it more comfortable to carry.

Materials

- One 3-foot section of 4-inch diameter pipe
- One 4-inch diameter flat end cap
- One large door hinge
- Six sets of nuts, bolts, and washers or six large rivets
- One 12-inch round, 3/8-inch thick piece of board
- One 12-inch round piece of camping mat
- Four feet of nylon strap

Instructions

Step 1

Cut the bottom end of the 4-inch diameter pipe at a 45-degree angle. This will allow the pipe to slide into the mud easier. Drill a small hole in the side of the pipe near the top to allow air into the pipe to make it easier to pull it out of the mud.

Step 2

Center the hinge on the end cap and mark the holes. Drill out the holes for the hinge.

Step 3

Attach the hinge to the seat using either nuts and bolts or washers and rivets. Glue the camping mat to the top of the seat.

This lightweight duck hunter's seat is ideal for marshes and swamps.

Step 4

Attach the hinge to the 4-inch end cap, again using either nuts and bolts or washers and rivets.

Step 5

Attach the nylon strap by looping it around the base of the seat or by pop-riveting it.

The seat flips up on a hinge for easier carry.

BACKREST

Hunters that spend a lot of time in open fields will appreciate this backrest. It allows you to rest your back against something when you're sitting on the ground. These lightweight supports can be very handy at outdoor concerts or picnics, as well.

Materials

- Two 23-inch sections of 3/4-inch diameter pipe
- Two 20-inch sections of 1/2-inch diameter pipe
- Two 14-inch sections of 1/2-inch diameter pipe
- One 7-inch section of 3/4-inch diameter pipe
- Two 2-inch sections of 1/2-inch diameter pipe
- Two 1/2-inch diameter T-connectors
- Four 3/4-inch diameter T-connectors
- Two 1/2-inch diameter 90-degree elbows
- Four feet of nylon strap

Instructions

Step 1

Attach two of the 3/4-inch T-connectors to the 7-inch section of 3/4-inch pipe; insert the pipe into the bottom openings. Insert 23-inch pipes into the side openings of both T-connectors.

Step 2

Attach the remaining two 3/4-inch T-connectors to the ends of the 23-inch pipes, inserting the pipes into the bottom openings. Line up the T-connectors so that you can look through both of them. Slide a 14-inch section of 1/2-inch diameter pipe through the T-connectors. The pipe should slide freely and extend out through the T-connectors to form the hinge at the top of the backrest.

A bare frame for the backrest.

Step 3

Attach a 1/2-inch diameter, 90-degree elbow to each end of the 14-inch long pipe. Attach a 20-inch section of 1/2-inch diameter pipe to the open ends of the 90-degree elbows. Slip the pipes into the side openings of two 1/2-inch diameter T-connectors.

Step 4

Connect the two T-connectors with the remaining 14-inch section of pipe.

The completed camouflage backrest, ready for action.

Step 5

Cut one end of each of the 2-inch sections of 1/2-inch diameter pipe at 45-degree angle. Insert the flat ends of the 2-inch pipes into the bottoms of the T-connectors. (This gives the rest something to bite into the dirt, making it a little more stable.)

Step 6

Attach the nylon strap to the bottom 14-inch pipe and the 7-inch pipe on the bottom of the back. This is used to adjust the angle of the backrest and keep it from sliding out from behind you. It also works as a carrying strap.

Options
The backrest can be padded in many different ways. Here are a couple of suggestions:
Weave the backrest with nylon webbing and pop rivet the ends to the pipe, as on a lawn chair. If you have the time and patience, the same thing could be done with para cord.
Cut a piece of camping mat to the inside dimensions of the backrest. Place the matting inside the backrest frame and duct tape the mat into place.
An additional piece of mat can be taped to the bottom of the backrest and laid flat when sitting. This will help to keep your No. 4 point of contact dry and more comfortable.

The hunter's seat frame completed and ready for webbing.

HUNTER'S SEAT

This small seat is designed to keep your backside off the ground and dry, as well as keeping you more comfortable. Though it looks heavy it actually is very light, weighing about 3 pounds.

The seat itself can be constructed from webbing or a

padded piece of plywood. Another option would be to simply duct tape a piece of camping mat in place, using it as a sort of webbing.

Materials

- Two 14-inch sections of 1 1/2-inch diameter pipe
- Two 11-inch sections of 1 1/2-inch diameter pipe
- Four 6-inch sections of 1 1/2-inch diameter pipe
- Four three-way 90-degree elbows for 1 1/2-inch pipe
- Four 1 1/2-inch diameter end caps

Instructions

Step 1
Insert a 6-inch pipe into the bottom opening on each of the three-way 90-degree elbows. Attach an end cap to each of the 6-inch pipes.

Step 2
Attach a three way 90-degree elbow to each end of the two 14-inch pipes

Step 3
Connect the two 14-inch pipes by inserting an 11-inch pipe into the open ends of the three-way 90-degree elbows.

BENCHREST TRIPOD

If you like punching holes in paper as much as I do, you know the only true way to achieve accuracy is with the aid of tripod or bipod. Well, we did shooting sticks for hunting in the first book, so this time we'll make a tripod for shooting from a bench.

Materials

- Three 12-inch sections of 1/2-inch diameter pipe
- One three-way 90-degree elbow for 1/2-inch pipe
- One rubber-coated, U-shaped utility hook
- Para cord

Instructions

Step 1

In the top outside bend of the elbow, drill a hole that is slightly smaller than the threads of the utility hook. Screw the hook into the hole.

Step 2

Drill a small hole in each of the 12-inch sections of 1/2-inch pipe. The hole should be drilled through one side of the pipe, one half inch from the end.

Step 3

Insert the undrilled ends of the three 12-inch sections of pipe into the openings on the three-way 90 degree elbow.

Step 4

Slip the end of a piece of para cord through the hole in one of the legs and tie a knot to secure the cord. Run the

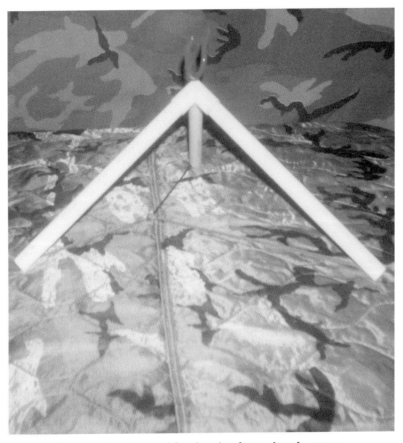

This tripod can be used for shooting from a bench or prone.

other end through the hole in another leg, pull it snug, and knot it. Run the remaining para cord from the third pipe, pull it snug, and tie it to center of the first para cord. This will keep the pipe rigid and prevent the legs of the tripod from sliding out when the weight of a firearm is placed in the hook.

ATLATL

The atlatl, or spear thrower, is one of the oldest hunting tools known to man, predating the bow and arrow by thousands of years. Originally the spear (properly called a dart) was made of wood or bamboo and tipped with a stone or bone point. The throwers were made of wood or antler, so we are taking a step of probably 20 thousand years by using PVC.

Materials

- One 48-inch section of 1/2-inch diameter CPVC pipe
- One 20-inch section of 1/2-inch diameter pipe
- One 1/2-inch diameter CPVC end cap
- A thin piece of flexible plastic (such as the plastic from a laundry soap bottle)
- Duct tape
- Leather bootlaces

Instructions

Dart construction
Step 1
Cut a notch in the end of the CPVC pipe approximately 1/2 inch long and wide enough to accept the leather laces. Use a hacksaw or a hobby tool with a cutting wheel.

Step 2
Starting from the notch you've just made cut another 6-inch long slot, just wide enough to accommodate the flexible plastic.

Step 3
Draw a one-piece pattern on a piece of flexible plastic

Preparing to launch the atlatl.

that resembles two oversized feathers. Mine measures six inches long. In the center of the feathers at the top and the bottom, draw a tab about 1/2-inch long and 1/2-inch wide. Cut out the feathers with the tabs attached.

Step 4
Insert the feather into the 6-inch cut in the CPVC. Center the feathers and duct tape the top and bottom tabs into place. A little contact cement won't hurt. Attach the CPVC end cap. It serves as a kind of blunt tip, plus puts additional weight forward making for a better cast when thrown. (Different points can be constructed for the dart; a sharpened dowel is shown in the photos.)

The atlatl is a hunting weapon that predates the bow.

Thrower construction
Step 1
Drill a hole half an inch from the end of the 20-inch section of 1/2-inch diameter pipe. Run a small piece of leather bootlace though and tie a small loop about an inch in diameter.

Step 2
Drill two holes at the opposite end, one approximately 5 inches from the end, the next just half an inch above the first hole. Drill the holes through both sides of the pipe. Run the leather bootlace though the bottom holes and back through the top holes. This will give you two loops, one on each side of the thrower. Adjust the size of the loops to snugly hold your thumb and forefinger. When this is done, tie a knot in the leather bootlace.

To use the atlatl, hold the thrower with your thumb and forefinger through the loops and fingers wrapped around the base. Lay the dart on top of the thrower. Set the notch of the dart into the 1-inch loop at the end of the thrower. Grasp the shaft of the dart with your thumb and forefinger. With a lobbing motion, bring your arm forward and release the shaft. It will take a lot of practice, and I recommend you seek more detailed information on their use, but atlatls are a lot of fun once you get the hang of them.

Note: Always keep safety in mind—you are launching a projectile that will fly farther than any hand-thrown spear. People and property should be kept at safe distance; one of my best throws went about 20 yards further than I had anticipated and cleared a 6-foot fence, damn near killing my neighbor's camper. So be careful!

Slip the loop at the end of the launcher into the notch on the dart to load.

SPOTTING SCOPE STOCK

Due to the high level of magnification, most spotter scopes are about impossible to use without a tripod or rest of some sort. Mounting a spotter scope to a stock gives you a quick and stable platform without the hassle of messing with a tripod.

Materials

- Two 12-inch sections of 1/2-inch diameter pipe
- Two 2 1/2-inch sections of 1/2-inch diameter pipe
- One 1 1/2-inch section of 1/2-inch diameter pipe
- Two 1/2-inch diameter T-connectors
- Two 1/2-inch diameter 90-degree elbows
- One 1/2-inch diameter end cap
- One bolt or screw that is the same diameter and thread as your spotting scope

Instructions

Step 1
Attach a 90-degree elbow to each of the 12-inch sections of pipe.

Step 2
Attach a T-connector to the opposite end of each 12-inch pipe.

Step 3
Insert a 2 1/2-inch pipe into the open end of each 90-degree elbow.

Step 4
Set the 90-degree elbow of one pipe opposite the

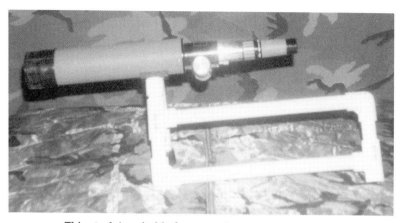

This stock is suitable for a spotting scope or a camera.

The stock can be wrapped in cammo tape if desired.

T-connector of the other pipe. Insert the 2 1/2-inch pipe that extends from the elbow into the T-connector. This should give you a rectangular frame.

Step 5

Insert the 1 1/2-inch pipe into one of the open T-connectors.

Step 6

Drill a hole in the end cap. Insert the screw or bolt that matches the threads of the spotter scope through the hole and screw it to the scope.

Step 7

Attach the end cap to the stock frame. It is best not to cement the end cap.

SHOOTING BENCH

A steady rest is essential to accurate shooting. One of the best ways to accomplish this is to shoot from a shooting bench. Here is a cheap, easy-to-build bench for just that purpose.

Materials

- Two 36-inch sections of 1 1/2-inch diameter pipe
- Four 16-inch sections of 1 1/2-inch diameter pipe
- Eight 14-inch sections of 1 1/2-inch diameter pipe
- Four 1 1/2 inch diameter T-connectors
- Two four-way 1 1/2-inch diameter 90-degree elbows
- Four 1 1/2-inch diameter flat end caps (Note: get the deepest caps you can find.)
- Four 1/2-inch diameter bolts with nuts and washers
- One sheet of 3/8- or 1/2-inch plywood, 40x40 inches

Instructions

Step 1

Insert the ends of a 36-inch section of pipe into the bottom openings of two of the T-connectors.

Step 2

Insert a 14-inch long pipe into each of the remaining openings of the two T-connectors. It should now look like a large letter "I."

Step 3

On one side of the "I" attach a T-connector to the 14-inch pipes. Insert the pipes into the bottom opening. Rotate the T-connector so that the side openings are vertical.

Step 4

On the other end of the large "I" attach a four-way 90-degree elbow to each of the 14-inch pipe. Attach at one of the bottom openings. With both elbows installed insert the remaining 36-inch pipe. This should complete the base for the bench.

Step 5

Insert a 16-inch pipe into the bottoms of the two vertical T-connectors. Do the same on the bottoms of the two four-way 90-degree elbows.

Step 6

Insert 14-inch pipes into the remaining top openings of the T-connectors and elbows.

Step 7

Center the plywood on top of the frame to determine where each pipe meets the plywood. Mark the center in each of the four corners and drill a hole. Insert a bolt or screw into each hole.

Step 8

Drill a hole in the tops of the four end caps. On the opposite side of the plywood attach each of the end caps using a washer and nut.

Step 9

Determine how much relief you want to take from the plywood and remove it. This will make shooting more comfortable, allowing you to sit somewhat inside the benchrest.

Step 10

Attach the plywood to the frame using the end caps.

Shooting bench ready for the field.

The support frame for the shooting bench.

RELOADING/WORK BENCH

A steady bench for work or reloading is a handy item to have. Constructing the reloading bench is done in much the same manner as the shooting bench. The only difference is that since there's no cutout area, we'll use more of the four-way 90-degree elbows and heavier plywood. Also, to make it steadier, fill the legs of the bench with sand.

Materials

- Three 36-inch sections of 1 1/2-inch diameter pipe
- Four 16-inch sections of 1 1/2-inch diameter pipe
- Eight 14-inch sections of 1 1/2-inch diameter pipe
- Two 1 1/2-inch diameter T-connectors
- Four four-way 1 1/2-inch diameter 90-degree elbows
- Four 1 1/2-inch diameter flat end caps (Note: get the deepest caps you can find.)
- Four 1/2-inch diameter bolts with nuts and washers
- One sheet of 5/8- or 3/4-inch plywood, 40x40 inches

Instructions

Step 1
Insert a 36-inch long pipe into the bottom openings of two of the T-connectors.

Step 2
Insert a 14-inch long pipe into each of the remaining openings of the two T-connectors. It should look like a large letter "I."

Step 3
On each end of the "I," attach four-way 90-degree elbows. Insert the pipes into the side openings.

The bench frame shown without the top.

A completed bench.

Step 4

With all of the elbows installed, insert the remaining 36-inch pipes, attaching them at the other side opening. This should complete the base for the bench.

Step 5

Insert four 16-inch pipes into the bottoms of the vertical four-way 90-degree elbows.

Step 6

Insert 14-inch pipes in the remaining top openings of the elbows.

Step 7

Center the plywood on top of the frame to determine where each pipe comes up to meet the plywood. Mark the center in each of the four corners and drill a hole. Insert a bolt or screw into each hole.

Step 8

Drill a hole in the top of the four end caps. On the opposite side of the plywood attach each of the end caps using a washer and nut.

Step 9

Attach the plywood to the frame using the end caps.

HUNTING BLIND

Without a doubt one of the most effective ways to get close to game is to use a blind. This lightweight blind is very similar to those costing $100+. It is simple to construct and easy to carry. When constructed to these specifications it measures 5 feet tall and 8 feet in diameter at the base—big enough for a hunter or photographer and his or her gear.

Materials

- Four 7-foot sections of 1-inch diameter pipe
- Four 2-inch sections of 1-inch diameter pipe (spacers)
- Four 1-inch diameter T-connectors
- Four 1-inch diameter 45-degree elbows
- Four small "S" hooks
- Para cord
- Camouflage netting or material

Instructions

Step 1

Drill a small hole in one end of each 7-foot pipe. Loop an "S" hook to each pipe through the hole. This end will be at the bottom of the blind.

Step 2

Insert a 2-inch spacer into each of the openings on the four-way T-connector. Attach a 45-degree elbow to each spacer with the elbow pointing down.

Step 3

Insert the top end of each pipe into a 45-degree elbow. This should give you a pyramid-like structure.

The framework of the hunting blind.

Step 4

Tie a length of para cord from one "S" hook to the "S" hook directly across from it to form an "X" at the bottom of the blind. This is to help prevent the legs of the blind from slipping out once the weight of the cover is added.

Step 5

Drape the frame with camouflage netting or material and cut it to fit. Once the fit is determined, tie downs can be sewn or glued to the cover and in turn tied to the frame.

Optional Step 6

If wind will be an issue, drill another hole in the bottom of the pipes and run a loop of para cord through the hole. Stake the loop to the ground.

The hunting blind covered in mosquito netting.

BRUSH BOW

I love old-world technology, and archery is a big part of it. I have attempted to craft many bows over the years with the same results—kindling.

So, I figured, why not try the trusty PVC pipe? This little bow draws 35 pounds at 27 inches of draw, just right for recreation and occasional small-game hunting. Draw weight will vary from bow to bow, so don't be afraid to experiment. Its short length makes it great for hunting the brush where small-game animals like to hang out.

Warning: Remember that this is a bow and is capable of serious—even deadly—consequences if not respected.

Materials

- One 44-inch section of 1/2-inch diameter pipe
- One leather thong
- Spray foam insulation
- Tape

Instructions

Step 1

Spray the foam insulation into the pipe.

Step 2

Drill a small hole half an inch from each end of the pipe.

Step 3

Measure to determine the center of the bow, then mark two inches above the center. Start wrapping the tape around the bow, covering enough pipe to serve as a comfortable handhold.

Step 4

Insert the leather thong into one of the holes and tie a knot.

Step 5

Run the other end of the thong through the other hole. Flex the bow until the distance from the back of the bow to the string measures 5 or 6 inches. Knot the thong.

The author with his brush bow and an old roasting pan the arrow penetrated at a distance of 45 feet.

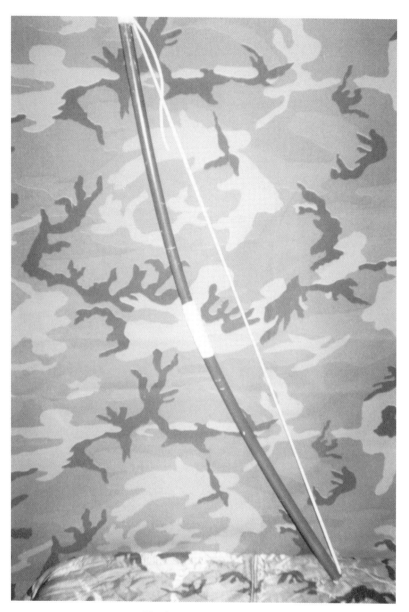

The finished brush bow.

Fishing

FISHING POLE

With fish finders and all that fancy newfangled stuff, it's easy to forget that half the fun of fishing is just taking it easy. Here is a low-tech fishing pole that will hopefully bring back those long-gone lazy summer days.

The PVC cane-style fishing pole can be made of a single piece of pipe or two shorter ones fitted together. The instructions here are for the two-piece pole.

Materials

- Two 4-foot sections of 3/4-inch diameter pipe

- Two 3/4-inch diameter end caps
- One coupler
- Two small roll pins or cotter pins
- Fishing lure swivel

Instructions

Step 1

Drill a small hole in one of the end caps. Insert the round end of the fishing lure swivel through the hole. Run a roll pin through the hole in the swivel. Cement the end cap into place on one of the pipes. (This will give you a permanent point to attach your fishing line.)

Step 2

Attach the other end cap to the remaining pipe. Do not cement it into place; you want to be able to take this apart. You can use this pipe to store your extra hook, line, and sinkers.

Step 3

Cement the coupler to the pipe. Attach the other pipe to the coupler. Drill a small hole through the pipe and coupler. When the pole is assembled, place the other roll pin in the hole. This will keep the pole together when you land the big one.

The fishing pole can be constructed in two pieces to make it more portable.

FISH GAFF

A fish gaff can be very handy when fishing through the ice since it's damn tough to put a 2-foot wide landing net through an 8-inch hole.

Materials

- One 20-inch section of 3/4-inch diameter pipe
- Two 3/4-inch diameter end caps
- Para cord
- One 8-inch piece of 3/16-inch diameter steel rod
- JB Weld

Instructions

Step 1

Drill a 3/16-inch diameter hole in each end cap.

Step 2

Run a length of para cord through one of the end caps. Make a loop large enough to get your hand through. Cement the end cap to the 20-inch long pipe. If you want, you can wrap para cord around the pipe to give it a handle. Or slip a bicycle handle over the pipe.

Step 3

Bend the first 1/2-inch of the 3/16-inch diameter steel rod at a right angle. Insert the steel rod into the other end cap. Stop at the bend. Bend the bottom four inches or so of the steel rod, forming a hook. Sharpen the hook with a file or grinder.

Step 4

Fill the end cap with JB Weld, making sure to cover the bent end inside the cap. Attach it to the 20-inch pipe.

A fishing gaff is a useful tool when ice fishing.

RAFT POLE

This is a good thing to have if you like to raft or canoe in waters that have shallow areas. By building it in two pieces it can be easily stored in the bottom of the raft or canoe. On this one we will use both a wooden dowel and foam insulation to help reinforce the pole.

Materials

- Two 4-foot sections of 1 1/2-inch diameter pipe
- Two 1 1/2-inch diameter end caps
- One 1 1/2-inch diameter end caps
- One 2-foot section of 1 1/2-inch diameter wood dowel
- Spray foam insulation
- Coupler

Instructions

Step 1

Insert the wooden dowel halfway into one end of one the 4-foot pipes. If you sand, don't take off too much—you want a good, tight fit. Attach the coupler at this end.

Step 2

From the open end fill the pipe with spray-foam insulation. Once this is dry, clean up the end of the pipe and cement the end cap.

Step 3

Insert some old newspaper or cloth into one end of the other 4-foot pipe. Push it as close to one foot into the pipe as possible. Spray in foam insulation from the opposite end. Once the insulation dries remove the cloth or newspaper. This will leave room for the wooden dowel. Attach the end cap on the end with the insulation.

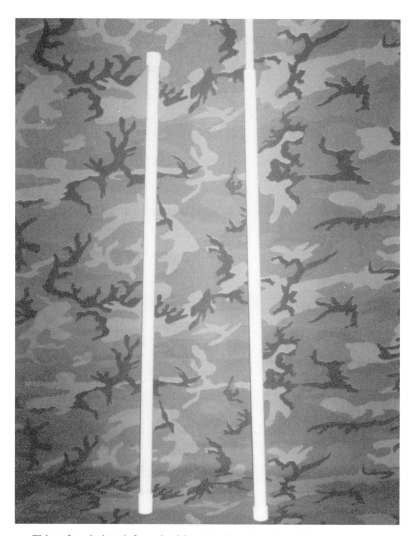

This raft pole is reinforced with a wooden dowel and foam insulation.

Step 4

Attach the two pipes at the coupler. Tape or para cord a handhold on one end.

BOW-FISHING REEL

Bow fishing for rough fish is a favorite pastime of mine. Stalking along the shoreline in search of carp is a great way to spend an afternoon. This bow reel was made out of necessity when I lost my old reel. It works as well as the store-bought one and was about 1/20th the cost.

Materials

- One 4-inch diameter end cap
- One piece of mild steel bar
- Two small "L" brackets
- Pop rivets

Instructions

Step 1
Place the two "L" brackets opposite one another on the inside of the 4-inch end cap. Mark the holes in the bracket and drill.

Step 2
Once the holes are drilled, line up the brackets and pop rivet them into place.

Step 3
Bend the mild steel bar to fit the contour of the bow's riser. Get it to fit as close as possible.

Step 4
Place the reel on the steel rod and mark the bracket holes. Once the holes are marked drill them out. Pop rivet the reel to the steel bar.

A bow-fishing reel attached to a compound bow.

Step 5

Tape the reel to the bow. Tie your line to the bow and wrap the line around the end cap.

FILET KNIFE HANDLE AND SHEATH

This is a neat little practical evening project. Using a good blade you can build a knife that floats. Or it can be used as the popular survival-type with the hollow handle.

The blade is up to you—either purchase a blade with a short tang or salvage the blade from a lock-blade knife. Just make sure it will fit into the PVC pipe sheath (if you decide to use one). This is the only time we will use thin-walled PVC pipe.

Materials

- One knife blade
- One 5-inch section of 1-inch diameter pipe
- One 1-inch diameter thin-walled pipe long enough to contain the knife blade
- Two 1-inch diameter end caps
- One 1-inch diameter coupler
- Para cord
- JB Weld

Instructions

Step 1

Fill one end of the 5-inch long pipe with JB Weld or a similar epoxy. Fill the pipe with enough epoxy to cover the knife's tang.

Step 2

Insert the tang of the knife and make sure that is straight. Let the epoxy set up.

Step 3

Drill a hole in one of the end caps. Insert the para cord

The filet knife and sheath.

and make a loop large enough to put your hand through comfortably. Attach the end cap to the 5-inch pipe. You now have a finished handle.

Step 4

Attach the coupler to the pipe to be used as the sheath. Drill a hole in the side of the pipe and insert a length of para cord. Tie a loop to put the sheath on your belt. Attach the other end cap to the opposite end.

Shelters

PICK-UP SHELTER

This shelter, similar to a tarp-and-bow system on military trucks, is great for the pickup owner who doesn't like to sleep on the ground. Building it costs about $15—a bargain compared to similar premade shelters that run around $150. The name-brand model I priced had all the whistles and bells but was the same basic design. With the PVC shelter you can make it as fancy as you like and still be money ahead.

Materials

- Six 46-inch sections of 1/2-inch diameter pipe
- Two 41-inch sections of 1/2-inch diameter pipe

- One 1/2 inch diameter four-way T-connector
- Two 1/2-inch diameter three-way T-connectors
- Three 8-inch long 1/2-inch diameter wooden dowels
- One large tarp
- Para cord

Instructions

Step 1
Slide an 8-inch wooden dowel through the side openings of each of the T-connectors. These will act as internal couplers.

Step 2
Attach the 46-inch pipes to each of the T-connectors, slipping them over the 8-inch wooden dowels.

Step 3
Place the ends of the 46-inch pipes into the stake pockets on each side of the pickup box, putting the pipes with the four-way T-connector in the center. These will be our bows. This requires bending the 46-inch pipes, which places stress on the pipe at the T-connectors. If you do not use the wooden dowels either the connectors will break or the pipes will pop out of the sockets.

Step 4
Attach a 41-inch pipe to each T-connector to connect the bows.

Step 5
Place the tarp over the bows and cut it to fit. Then tie the tarp to the stake pockets.

Step 6
Once the tarp is cut to fit, tape or glue a skirt to the tarp above the box of the pickup, long enough to drape over the sides; this will shed the rain to the outside of the pickup box.

The materials for this PVC pickup truck shelter frame cost a fraction
of the price of a store-bought model.

DOME SHELTER

Here is an easy-to-make shelter for one person that goes together in no time. When complete it measures 80-inches in diameter and is 38-inches high.

Materials

- Two 10-foot sections of 1/2-inch diameter pipe
- Two S-hooks
- One large tarp
- Two 80-inch lengths of para cord

Instructions

Step 1
Drill a small hole 1 inch from the end of each pipe.

Step 2
Slip a piece of para cord through the holes at one end of each pipe.

Step 3
Tie an S-hook to the other end of each piece of para cord.

Step 4
Place the pipes on top of one another at the center of each pipe.

Step 5
Bend the top pipe and attach the S-hook to the end of the pipe by inserting the hook into the hole. Do the same with the bottom pipe. After you've bent both pipes into arches, lash them together where they meet.

The no-frills one-man dome shelter.

Step 6

Place the tarp over the frame and cut or fold it to fit. If you fold the tarp to the inside of the shelter it will serve as a floor or simply a moisture barrier. The shelter can be anchored by staking down the ends of the pipe or placing a rock on the tarp.

WALL TENT

Wall tents are nice because their design allows for lots of usable space. Tents like this one have become very expensive over the years, with the cost of the framework alone starting at $200.

This wall tent has the potential to be used for things other than just a tent. If you desire you could cover it with heavy-duty clear plastic and make a neat portable greenhouse. Or use it for storing lawn and garden tools or as a garage for an all-terrain vehicle. With a little work and imagination the frame could be sided with 1/4-inch plywood and made into a rigid shelter for a more permanent storage facility.

Materials

- Eight 5-foot sections of 1 1/2-inch diameter pipe
- Five 3-foot sections of 1 1/2-inch diameter pipe
- Eight 2-inch 1 1/2-inch diameter pipe spacers
- Two 1 1/2-inch diameter T-connectors
- Two 1 1/2-inch diameter four-way 90-degree connectors
- Four 1 1/2-inch diameter 45-degree connectors
- Two 1 1/2-inch diameter three-way 90-degree connectors
- Eight 1 1/2-inch diameter threaded couplers (male)
- Four 1 1/2-inch diameter threaded couplers (female)
- Nylon tarp for cover

Instructions

Step 1

Begin construction by framing the entrance to the tent. First, attach one of the side openings of a T-connector to the end of a 3-foot long pipe.

Front view of the wall tent frame.

Step 2

Insert a spacer into the other side opening of the T-connector.

Step 3

Attach a 45-degree connector to the end of the spacer.

Step 4

Insert a spacer into the open end of the 45-degree connector.

Side view of the wall tent frame.

Step 5
Attach a female end coupler to the end of the spacer.

Step 6
Insert a spacer into the remaining opening of the T-connector.

Detail of the rear corner post.

Step 7

Attach a threaded female coupler to the spacer. Repeat steps 1 through 7 for the other side of the entrance.

Step 8

Next you'll construct the poles for the rear of the tent.

With the tarp in place, you can mark where the grommets will go.

Begin by attaching a four-way 90-degree connector to the end of a 3-foot long pipe.

Step 9

Insert a spacer into the end of the four-way 90-degree connector opposite from the 3-foot long pipe.

The rear view of the finished tent shows the tarp folded in a style similar to gift wrapping on a box. (No, I can't wrap presents worth a darn either.)

Step 10

Attach a 45-degree connector to the end of the spacer.

Step 11

Insert a spacer into the open end of the 45-degree connector.

Step 12

Attach a female end coupler to the end of the spacer.

Step 13

Insert a spacer into one of the remaining openings on the four-way 90-degree connector.

Step 14

Attach a female threaded coupler onto the spacer. Repeat steps 8 through 14 for the other rear tent pole.

Step 15

Now attach male threaded couplers to the ends of seven of the 5-foot pipes and also to the end of the remaining piece of 3-foot long pipe.

Step 16

Build the side walls of the tent by screwing two of the 5-foot pipes into the female couplers on the front wall poles.

Step 17

On the rear wall poles, insert the ends of the 5-foot pipes into the unthreaded openings of the four-way 90-degree connectors.

Step 18

Screw the male threaded end of one 5-foot pipe into the horizontal threaded female coupler on one rear wall pole. Attach a coupler to the end of the 5-foot pipe.

Step 19

Screw the male threaded end on the 3-foot pipe into the horizontal threaded female coupler on the other rear wall pole. Connect the 3-foot pipe to the 5-foot pipe at the coupler.

Step 20

Screw the male threaded end of two 5-foot pipes into the female threaded couplers at the top of each rear wall pole.

Step 21

Create a ridge pole for the top of the tent by attaching a three-way 90-degree connector to each end of a 5-foot pipe.

Step 22

Attach the three-way 90-degree connectors to the ends of the 5-foot pipes coming up from the four corners.

Step 23

To help steady the tent, run a rope along the pipes and tie it off at the couplers. This will make it more rigid and prevent the non-threaded pipe ends from slipping out of the couplers.

Step 24

Drape a large nylon tarp over the frame and begin to fit it to the frame. Once the tarp is fitted, mark the lashing points and add grommets.

Step 25

With the grommets added to the tarp, secure the tarp to the frame.

Camping Gear

LANTERN HOLDER

A lantern holder is a handy item for camping. I don't like to set lanterns on the ground or even a stump, for that matter, as it is just too easy to tip them over. Also, hanging the lantern off the ground allows for greater light dispersion.

Materials

- Three 5-foot sections of 1-inch diameter pipe
- One 1-inch three-way elbow
- One small snaplink
- One small eyebolt
- A short length of chain

Instructions

Step 1

Drill a small hole in the bottom of the three-way elbow. Screw the hook or eyebolt into the hole and attach the chain.

Step 2

Insert the three 5-foot sections of pipe into the three-way elbow.

Step 3

Snaplink the lantern handle to the chain.

Options

Cut the bottom of each 5-foot pipe at an angle, creating a point. This will allow you to stick the poles into the ground to make the structure more stable. If you do not have a three-way elbow, build a simple tripod using your 5-foot pipes. Secure the tops with a small length of thin chain. Try to stay away from string or cord, as these can get hot and melt or even catch on fire.

TENT STAKE

OK, everyone knows you can't use plastic stakes in rocky ground—you have to use steel. But for those times that you're not camping on the edge of Mount Everest you can get by with plastic. Just go to your local outdoors store and you will find all kinds of plastic tent stakes. But most of them won't last as long as these and will cost a hell of a lot more.

Materials

- One 1-foot section of 1-inch diameter pipe
- One small S-hook

Instructions

Step 1

Cut the end of the pipe at a 45- or 60-degree angle.

Step 2

Drill a hole 1/2-inch from the top of the pipe. Slip the S-hook through the hole. Use the S-hook to grip the stake loops on the outside of the tent.

Option

Whip up a batch of JB Weld and fill the top end of the pipe. This will prevent the "S" hook from swiveling, but will make the stake a bit more durable if you have to pound it into hard ground.

Two different styles of PVC tent stake.

CHAPTER 6

Cheap Living

GUN RACK

This gun rack is a handy item for keeping your long guns out of the way. Actually it would also work well for fishing rods, bows, or even as a hat or coat rack.

Materials

- One 22-inch section of 1/2 inch diameter pipe
- Four 12-inch sections of 1/2-inch diameter pipe
- Four 8-inch sections of 1/2-inch diameter pipe
- Two 4-inch sections of 1/2-inch diameter pipe

- Eight 1-inch sections of 1/2-inch diameter pipe (spacers)
- Six 1/2-inch diameter T-connectors
- Four 1/2-inch diameter 90-degree elbows
- Eight 1/2-inch diameter 45-degree elbows
- Two eyebolts

Instructions

Step 1
Insert the 22-inch pipe into the bottom openings of two T-connectors.

Step 2
Insert a 12-inch section of pipe into each of the remaining openings on the T-connectors. This should give you a large "I" shape.

Step 3
Attach 90-degree elbows to each of the horizontal 8-inch pipes. Insert two more 8-inch pipes into the elbows at the top of the "I." Then attach the sides of two T-connectors to the open ends of those 8-inch pipes.

Step 4
Attach the remaining two 8-inch pipes to the other side openings of the T-connectors. Attach another T-connector to the open end of each 8-inch pipe.

Step 5
Attach the 4-inch pipe to the bottom opening of the T-connector. Slide the 4-inch sections of pipe into the 90-degree elbows at the bottom of the rack. The open bottom ends of the four T-connectors should be facing toward you.

This gun or fishing-pole rack is ready for painting, or can be hung as is.

Side view of the hooks.

Step 6

Insert 1-inch spacers into the open ends of the four T-connectors.

Step 7

Attach four 45-degree elbows to the spacers, then add four more spacers, followed by the remaining four 45-degree elbows. Note: The hooks on the rack can be made deeper by adding an additional spacer and possibly an end cap. Also, the hooks can be wrapped in tape or moleskin to prevent scratching the finish of the guns or fishing rods.

Step 8

Drill two holes in the top of the rack and attach the eyebolts.

CHAIR

This PVC chair would be a good companion to the shooting bench, garage, or even around the kitchen table.

Materials

- Eight 14-inch sections of 1 1/2-inch diameter pipe
- Two 16-inch sections of 1 1/2-inch diameter pipe
- Two four-way 90-degree connectors
- Two three-way 90-degree connectors
- Six 1 1/2-inch diameter end caps

Instructions

Step 1
Build a square seat out of four 14-inch sections of pipe by connecting them with two four-way 90-degree connectors for the back of the seat and two three-way 90-degree connectors for the front. (The open ends of the three-way connectors should be pointing down.)

Step 2
Insert the remaining four 14-inch sections of pipe into the bottom openings of the connectors to make the legs. Attach the end caps. If the chair is going to be used indoors, glue felt pads to the end caps to protect the floor and help prevent the chair from sliding.

Step 3
Insert the 16-inch pipes into the two remaining openings on the four way 90-degree elbows for the back rest. Attach the end caps.

PVC chair ready to be finished with webbing or a piece of plywood for the seat.

Options

The seat of the chair can be done with nylon webbing or by padding a piece of wood and attaching it. The back can be done the same way.

SHOWER-CURTAIN ROD OR CLOSET ROD

This is a very easy project. The only thing you'll need other than the materials listed below are two opposing walls. PVC that's 1-inch or larger is pretty stout stuff, but it could be reinforced by inserting a wooden dowel. I would not use it at all, however, for a large closet where the rod would be longer than 5 feet long. (A shower curtain will not be taxed nearly as much.)

Materials

- One piece of 1-inch diameter pipe. The length will depend of the size of the area to be covered.
- Two 1-inch diameter end caps

Instructions

Step 1
Measure the space between the walls and cut the 1-inch diameter pipe to length. It may have to be shortened, but only slightly.

Step 2
Determine the height of the rod and attach the end caps on the opposing walls.

Step 3
Insert the pipe into one of the end caps. Flex the pipe and insert the opposite end into the other end cap. If this doesn't work, try cutting the end cap in half and setting the pipe into it.

FLAG POLE

A house just ain't a home without a flag pole.

Materials

- One 8-foot section of 2-inch diameter pipe
- One 5-foot section of 2-inch diameter pipe
- One 2-inch diameter coupler (a long one if possible)
- One small pulley
- One rope cleat
- One eyebolt
- Rope

Instructions

Step 1

Attach the rope cleat to the 8-foot pipe using screws or pop rivets. It should be located a foot or so from the top end of the pipe.

Step 2

Dig a 3-foot deep hole and insert the bottom end of the 8-foot section of 2-inch diameter pipe. Fill in the hole around the pipe. Put the remaining dirt in the pipe to help steady it.

Step 3

Attach the 2-inch diameter coupler. An option at this point would be to insert a wooden or metal interior coupler as well.

Step 4

Attach the 2-inch diameter end cap to the 5-foot section of 2-inch diameter pipe.

Flag pole.

Step 5

Drill a small hole into the end cap and attach the pulley using the eyebolt.

Step 6

Lace the rope through the pulley and attach the 5-foot pipe to the coupler.

BOUNDARY MARKER

This idea is by no means my own. I have seen construction companies use these for years in parking lots to protect propane tanks or air conditioners from careless motorists. Many times they are filled with sand or concrete.

I live on the edge of town on a street with no curb. The corner of my property continues to erode to traffic, so I installed a single post barrier.

Materials

- One four-foot section of 1 1/2-inch diameter pipe
- One 1 1/2-inch diameter end cap
- Reflective tape

Instructions

Step 1
Dig a 1-foot deep hole and insert the pipe.

Step 2
Fill in the hole and attach the end cap. Put any leftover dirt inside the pipe to help keep it in place. Wrap the pole with reflective tape.

A boundary marker in place at the end of the driveway.

ROPE/CORD RACK

If you are like me and hate tangled ropes and electrical cords, this will save you a lot of grief. It allows you to neatly store ropes and such, keeping them out of the way and ready for use. The clothespins hold the ends of the cords or ropes in place.

Materials

- Two 10-inch sections of 1/2-inch diameter pipe
- Two 14-inch sections of 1/2-inch diameter pipe
- Four 1/2-inch diameter T-connectors
- One 1-inch long 1/2-inch diameter spacer
- One 1/2-inch diameter end cap
- One eyebolt
- Two clothespins

Instructions

Step 1
Attach a T-connector to each end of the 10-inch long pipes. Use bottom opening.

Step 2
Make a rectangle by sliding the 14-inch pipes into the side openings of the T-connectors.

Step 3
Insert the 1-inch spacer into one of the openings on one T-connector.

Step 4
Drill a hole in the 1/2-inch end cap. Insert the eyebolt. Attach the end cap to the spacer.

Step 5
Tape or glue the two clothespins to the 14-inch pipe.

This lightweight rack will help keep your electrical cords
or lengths of rope from becoming tangled.

RACK FOR DRYING CLOTHES

Seems like half the clothes you buy anymore can't be dried in a dryer. Between the wife's sweaters and my polypropylene we were left with no other option but to make something that would dry these things. Sure, you can hang them on a clothesline, but that's not real handy when it's 25 degrees below zero.

One day I after laying out my polyprop on every available surface in the house it dawned on me. I took a PVC target stand and made some slight changes that allowed us to drape clothes over it. (Those of you who have read the first PVC book may remember this project.)

Materials

- Three 36-inch sections of 1-inch diameter pipe
- Four 20-inch sections of 1-inch diameter pipe
- Four 14-inch sections of 1-inch diameter pipe
- Two 2-inch sections of 1-inch diameter pipe (spacers)
- Six 1-inch diameter T-connectors
- Two 1-inch diameter elbows
- Four 1-inch diameter end caps

Instructions

Step 1
Insert 14-inch pipes into both side openings of two of the T-connectors. Attach end caps to the open ends of the pipe.

Step 2
Insert a spacer into the bottom opening of the T-connectors.

Rack for drying clothes.

Step 3

Using the side openings, slide T-connectors over each spacer.

Step 4

Slide a section of 36-inch pipe into the bottom openings of the T-connectors, joining the two sections of pipe.

Step 5

Insert 20-inch pipes into the side openings of the T-connectors. Using the side openings, attach T-connectors to the open end of the pipe.

Step 6

Connect the bottom openings of the T-connectors with a 36-inch section of pipe.

Step 7

Insert a 20-inch pipe into the openings of the T-connectors. Attach an elbow to the open end of each 20-inch pipe.

Step 8

Connect the elbows with a section of 36-inch pipe.

COVERS FOR ROPE HANDLES

Rope makes great handles, but if there is a real amount of weight to the crate, the rope bites into your hands. If you have ever carried heavy crates (such as ammo crates) that have rope handles you will appreciate this little deal.

Materials

- One length of 3/4-inch diameter pipe (the length will depend on the size of the rope handle)
- Duct tape

Instructions

Step 1
Using a hobby tool or hacksaw cut the pipe length-ways.

Step 2
Slip the pipe over the rope with the sliced side up.

Step 3
Wrap the tape around the pipe

EMERGENCY FIX FOR A WOODEN HANDLE

One thing that flat make me mad is to be digging or sweeping and have the handle on a shovel or broom break. Here is a quick way to get back up and running until you can get to the hardware store. Basically what we are doing is placing a splint on the break just like for a broken bone.

Materials

- One 10-14-inch section of pipe
- Duct tape
- Three hose clamps

Instructions

Step 1

Split the pipe using a hacksaw or hobby tool.

Step 2

Match up the broken pieces and place a one half of the pipe on each side.

Step 3

Either duct tape or hose clamp the pipe into place over the break.

Option

Drill two small holes through the pipe and handle. Insert a screw or bolt and cinch it down.

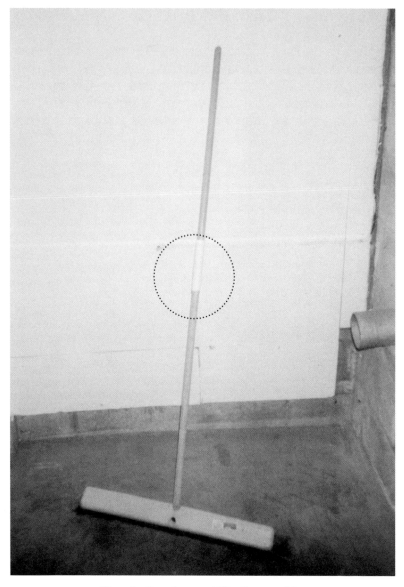

They don't make wood like they used to.
Broom handle repaired with PVC pipe

DIGGING STICK

This is another of my favorite projects—simple, effective, and using technology as old as man himself. Used for digging roots, flint, and everything else, this is one tool that will not let you down. It can be used for digging holes for traps, prospecting, or even digging up dandelions in the front yard. In a pinch it can even be used for self-defense.

Materials

- One 12- to 36-inch section of 1-inch diameter pipe
- One 1-inch diameter end cap
- Para cord (optional)

Instructions

Step 1
Determine the length of the stick. Measure 6 inches back from one of the ends and mark it.

Step 2
Using a hacksaw or hobby tool cut the pipe at an angle from the mark to the end. This should give a pointed end. A commando or finger saw works real well for this.

Step 3
Attach the end cap and wrap the handle with para cord.

One of man's oldest tools—the digging stick.

ANIMAL PEN

Many people raise rabbits, chickens, or in my case, ducks. The PVC pen is an easy-to-build and lightweight way to keep them. I built one three years ago and am still using it today.

Materials

- Four 40-inch sections of 1/2-inch diameter pipe
- Eight 36-inch sections of 1/2-inch diameter pipe
- Four 1/2-inch diameter three-way elbows
- Roll of chicken wire
- Sixteen hose clamps

Instructions

Step 1
First make two rectangles. For each one, use four three-way elbows to connect two sections of 40-inch pipe and two sections of 36-inch pipe.

Step 2
With the two rectangles complete, insert the remaining four 36-inch sections of pipe into the open right angle of each three-way elbow on the bottom rectangle.

Step 3
Attach the top rectangle to the bottom rectangle by slipping the three-way connectors over the 36-inch sections of pipe.

Step 4
Using two hose clamps, attach one end of the roll of chicken wire to the top 36-inch pipe on one end of the pen.

Duck at home in his PVC pen.

Step 5

Wrap the wire under the pen, creating a floor, and bring it up to the top 36-inch section of pipe on the opposite end. Secure it to the top with two hose clamps.

Step 6

Cut two lengths of chicken wire to cover the sides of the pen. Secure the wire on the sides with hose clamps. Wrap the clamp around the end wire panels as well to make it more sturdy and secure.

PET PICKET

For those of use who have pets, part of the enjoyment of having them is taking them with us on our travels outdoors. I have dogs, so when we go fishing or camping we picket them so they stay safe and can't roam around getting into trouble.

Materials

- One 18-inch section of 1-inch diameter pipe
- One 1-inch diameter end cap
- One eyebolt with two extra nuts
- Two large washers

Instructions

Step 1

Cut the pipe at one end at an angle (45 to 60 degrees will work).

Step 2

Place one washer in the end cap. Drill a hole through the end cap that lines up with the hole in the washer.

Step 3

JB Weld the other washer to the top of the end cap.

Step 4

Screw a nut onto the eyebolt all the way to the end of the threads.

Step 5

Insert the eyebolt into the cap. Screw a nut up to where it meets the washer, but not too tightly because we

Zeke is picketed in the yard.

want the eyebolt to be able to swivel. Then screw the last nut up solid to act as a stop.

Step 6

Cement the end cap onto to the pipe.

Step 7

Hammer the picket into the ground using a soft mallet such as those sold in camping stores. Strike the end cap, avoiding the eyebolt.

DIRT SIFTER

Unless you have spent some time trapping or prospecting you are probably wondering what you use a dirt sifter for. Well, trappers use them to delicately cover their traps with fine dirt and prospectors use them to separate the fine materials from the coarse.

Materials

- Four 1-foot sections of 1-inch diameter pipe
- Four 1-inch diameter elbows
- Screen

Instructions

Step 1

Connect the four 1-foot sections of pipe to the four elbows, creating a square frame.

Step 2

Lay the screen over the frame.

Step 3

Fold or roll the edges of the screen over, creating a seam along the edge. This will help to prevent the screen from tearing away from the frame. Pop rivet or screw the screen into place.

FIREWOOD CRADLE

Living where I do it's not a bad idea to keep some extra firewood close to the house. But if you store it on the ground it has a tendency to rot or become a haven for small, uninvited guests. This little wood cradle helps to alleviate these problems.

Materials

- Three 4-foot sections of 1 1/2-inch diameter pipe
- Six 14-inch sections of 1 1/2-inch diameter pipe
- Four 8-inch sections of 1 1/2-inch diameter pipe
- Four 1 1/2-inch diameter four-way 90-degree connectors
- Two 1 1/2-inch diameter three-way 90-degree connectors
- Two 1 1/2-inch diameter 90-degree elbows
- Four 1 1/2-inch diameter end caps

Instructions

Step 1
Create a rectangle using the side openings of the four-way 90-degree connectors, two 4-foot pipes, and two 14-inch pipes.

Step 2
Insert an 8-inch pipe into the bottom opening of each of the four four-way 90-degree connectors. Attach the end cap to the bottom of each 8-inch pipe.

Step 3
Insert a 14-inch long pipe into the top opening of each four-way 90-degree connector.

Step 4
Insert a 4-foot long pipe into the side opening of the three-way 90-degree connectors.

Step 5
Insert a 14-inch long pipe into the other side opening of the three-way 90-degree connectors.

Step 6
Attach a 90-degree elbow to each of the 14-inch long pipes

Step 7
Attach the open end of the connectors to the top of the 14-inch long pipes on the rectangle.

Firewood cradle.